ROCKS TELL STORIES

ROCKS TELL STORIES

SIDNEY HORENSTEIN

Beyond Museum Walls
The Millbrook Press
Brookfield, Connecticut

Cover: The colorful rock layers of the Grand Canyon
reveal much about Earth's history.
Photograph courtesy of Superstock.

Photographs on pp. 9 (top, #K13062), 35 (#K1762), and
54 (top, #K14819) courtesy of the Department of Library
Services, American Museum of Natural History.
All other photographs courtesy of Sidney Horenstein.

Library of Congress Cataloging-in-Publication Data

Horenstein, Sidney S.
Rocks tell stories / by Sidney Horenstein.
p.   cm. — (Beyond museum walls)
Includes bibliographical references (p.   ) and index.
Summary: Discusses the nature, significance, and uses of rocks,
how they can change over time, and what they can reveal about
the Earth and its history.
ISBN 1-56294-238-7 (lib. bdg.)
1. Petrology—Juvenile literature.   2. Rocks—Juvenile literature.
3. Geology—Juvenile literature.   [1. Rocks.   2. Petrology.
3. Geology.]   I. Title.   II. Series.
QE432.2H67   1993
552—dc20   92-16562   CIP   AC

Published by The Millbrook Press
2 Old New Milford Road
Brookfield, Connecticut 06804

Series editor: Margaret Cooper

CONTENTS

The granite in
these mountains
formed deep
below the Earth's
surface. Over
millions of years,
gradual wearing
away of the
surface rocks
has exposed
the granite.

ONE
ROCKS EVERYWHERE

Wherever you go, you see rocks. Mountains are made of rocks, and rocks lie under the Earth's plains and deserts, forests and oceans. Look around when you go walking. Along a stream you will probably see rocks below the water. You can often see rocks along stream banks, too.

You'll pass other good places to see rocks when you ride in a car or take the bus to school. Many roads have rock cliffs along their edges. These rock formations are called outcrops, and they are exposed because people had to cut through solid rock to make the road.

In cities, rocks are used for the walls of buildings, curbstones, and the paving on sidewalks. These rocks and others quarried from the Earth are usually called stones. *Dimension stones* are rocks cut or shaped in specific sizes. Architects determine the sizes when they draw the plans for a building, and they choose from a variety of colorful stones. At a quarry, large blocks of stone are cut out of the ground. The blocks are sent to a factory or mill where they are cut into the exact sizes called for by the architect.

Wherever you see rocks—in cities, in mountains, or along the roadside—they are pages of Earth's history. You can read those pages if you understand how rocks form and change over time.

MINERALS · A rock can be black or red or green or yellow—almost any color, in fact. Why do rocks have so many different colors? If you take a close look at a rock, you will usually see many specks in its surface. Often there are three or four different kinds of specks. The specks are bits of minerals, the building blocks of most kinds of rocks.

Minerals are solid substances that occur naturally but, unlike plants and animals, are not *organic*. Although about 3,000 minerals have been identified, only about 30 are important in identifying rocks. Rocks can be formed of one mineral, several minerals, or a combination of minerals and mineral-like substances—substances that occur naturally but do not have all the qualities of minerals. Coal, for example, is formed from ancient plants and therefore is not a mineral. But coal is classified as a kind of rock.

Each mineral has its own qualities, or properties. Color is one important property. Another is the way the mineral shines, or reflects light. Hardness is a third property. Many minerals are hard enough to scratch glass, but others are so soft that you can scratch them with your fingernail. Some minerals are clear enough to see through, but others are cloudy.

Other properties are not so easy to see. When heated, each mineral has a specific melting temperature. Each mineral has a chemical makeup that varies very little, no matter where it is found. And the atoms of each mineral are arranged in a geometric pattern. This pattern is repeated over and over, and it determines the shape, or *crystal form*, of the mineral. You rarely see the crystal forms of minerals in rocks because the minerals interfere with each other as the rock takes shape. Crystals form best in empty spaces, such as cavities in rocks.

The amount of each different mineral in a rock helps determine the rock's color and other characteristics. If most of the minerals in a rock are pink, then the rock will look pink. But rocks made of the

A beautiful example of the mineral tourmaline. Its crystal faces are well formed.

This granite solidified deep underground about one billion years ago. The pink mineral specks are feldspar; the black is hornblende; and the clear mineral is quartz.

same kinds and proportions of minerals may look quite different from each other if the sizes of the mineral specks are different. The specks may be large and easy to see, or they may be so small that you will not be able to see them without a powerful microscope. When you see a rock made of such small specks, you may think that it consists of only one mineral, when in fact several are present.

A fresh rock may also look different from one that has been exposed to the weather for a long time. Air and water can affect rocks, changing their minerals and thus their color. The outside of a rock then looks different from the inside. To see the true color of a rock, you sometimes have to break it open.

Once you understand what makes a rock a rock, you can begin to identify it and tell its origin. Most of what we know about the Earth's past comes from reading rocks. The minerals that make up a rock, its form, and its markings are all clues to events that may have happened millions of years ago.

Geologists—scientists who study the Earth—learn how to read rocks by studying what happens on Earth today. For example, if you visit a beach you may see markings on the sand made by plants, animals, waves, wind, and rain. Geologists know what made each kind of mark, and they know that most of them are found only on beaches. When they discover similar marks in rocks, they know that the rocks were once an ancient beach. When you think about the Earth, remember that the present is the key to the past.

TWO

THREE GROUPS OF ROCKS

All rocks fall into one of three groups. The name of each group describes how the rocks were formed.

IGNEOUS ROCKS ▪ *Igneous* rocks get their name from the Latin word for "fire," *ignis*. They were once molten (melted) material, called *magma*, that formed miles below the surface of the Earth, where the temperature is very high. Sometimes this material comes to the surface and forms volcanoes and *lava flows*. Volcanoes erupt because the molten material is full of gas under pressure. The gas escapes as the molten material comes to the surface, causing the eruption. Generally, the more gas that is released, the more violent the eruption. Sometimes the lava shoots out of the volcano so rapidly that it breaks into small pieces and solidifies in the air. Very small pieces of this lava are called volcanic ash, and large pieces are volcanic bombs.

Although lava begins to cool and harden into solid rock as soon as it reaches the air, it takes a long time for a thick lava flow to cool completely. The surface may seem to be cool and solid, but hot molten lava may still lie underneath the flow. Where the lava cools very quickly, it may form obsidian, a black and glassy rock. Pumice, a rock so light that it floats, forms when the lava is frothy with gas bubbles. And if the lava cools slowly, the mineral grains may be large

This lava flow formed irregular blocks as it cooled and cracked.

enough to see. Usually, however, lava and other volcanic rocks cool quickly, and the mineral grains are too small to see. Basalt, a dark rock, is the most common type of this lava. Igneous rocks are classified by the size of the mineral grains and the kinds of minerals they contain.

Not all molten material reaches the surface. Very often it cools and solidifies miles below. Geologists call this cooled material *plutonic* rock. While many volcanic rocks are dark, heavy, and fine-grained, plutonic rocks are lighter in color and weight, and they are coarse-grained. Granite is a common plutonic rock. It is made of several minerals, evenly distributed throughout the rocks. Quartz, one of the minerals in granite, is a combination of the elements silicon and oxygen. Most of the Earth's crust is made of silicon and oxygen combined with other elements.

You may wonder why you can see a rock such as granite, which formed deep in the Earth, at the surface. Granite provides an excellent example of the Earth's dynamism—its constantly changing nature. Granite can be seen on the surface because the crust of the Earth never remains stationary for long. Internal movements below the surface push part of the crust upward. Rivers, glaciers, wind, waves, and other forces of erosion wear away the covering rocks over millions of years, eventually exposing the granite.

SEDIMENTARY ROCKS ▪ The rocks that make up the second major group are called *sedimentary* rocks because they result from sediments, or deposits of materials, formed on the land or in the sea. Their important feature is that they are made of horizontal layers.

Here's a good way to understand layering. Get a clear plastic cup and two or three packages of sand of different colors. Pour sand of one color into the cup. This is your first layer. Pour a different color of sand into the cup, forming a second layer on top of the first one. That is exactly what happens in nature, except that streams and currents, not your hand, deposit the sand. The oldest layer—the one deposited first—is on the bottom of the pile, and the youngest layer lies on top.

In nature, as more layers are deposited the weight of the pile builds up, squeezing out water between the sediment particles. Minerals that were dissolved in the water are left behind and cement the particles together. When the spaces between particles are not completely filled with this mineral "cement," a sedimentary rock may crumble easily. But more cement may be added later as new water circulates through the spaces between the grains. Compaction, elimination of water, and cementation are the processes that convert loose sediment to harder sedimentary rock. In mountains, when you see horizontal layers that were formed in the sea, or when you see layers that are tilted, you know that Earth forces moved the rock.

Sedimentary rocks are divided into three smaller groups: clastic, biogenic, and chemical. *Clastic* sedimentary rocks, the first group, consist of particles of different sizes that come from the breakup of older rocks. The size of the particles determines a sediment's name. Clay feels smooth and is made of tiny particles too small to be seen. The particles of silt, the next size, are very small, too. Some geologists rub the particles on their fingernails or teeth to distinguish silt from clay. If they feel slightly gritty, the particles are silt. Clay and silt are also called mud.

Sand grains are large enough to be seen and have a gritty feel. The biggest sand grains are about $1/12$ inch (2 millimeters) in diameter. Gravel is larger than sand and is divided into pebbles, cobbles, and boulders. Boulders are particles larger than 10 inches (256 millimeters) in diameter.

Gravel, sand, silt, and clay are loose materials, or sediments. Even big boulders are considered sediment. Geologists call the layers

Sedimentary layers exposed in the Grand Canyon tell us about the ancient climate and geography of the area.

of loose particles unconsolidated rocks. When the loose particles become cemented together, they form consolidated rock. Geologists give different names to these rocks depending on what kind of particles they are made of. Rock made of hardened gravel is *conglomerate*, hardened sand is *sandstone*, hardened silt is *siltstone*, and hardened clay is *shale*.

Animals and plants are involved in the formation of certain rocks called *biogenic* sedimentary rocks. Shells of animals such as clams and snails sometimes accumulate on the sea floor in thick layers. Sometimes the layers are only an inch (2.5 centimeters) thick but they can also be 10 feet (3 meters) thick or more. Snails, clams, and many other animals without backbones that live in the ocean have a way of taking some of the plentiful calcium carbonate dissolved in seawater to make their shells, which are really external skeletons. The solid form of calcium carbonate is calcite, one of the Earth's common minerals. Sedimentary rocks made of calcite are called limestone. Pure limestone looks white because calcite is a white mineral, but sometimes other minerals are present that give the limestone different colors. For example, iron oxide gives limestone layers a brownish, yellowish, or even reddish color.

Coral reefs consist of the calcium carbonate skeletons made by huge colonies of tiny coral animals living together in tropical seas. Some reefs can be hundreds of miles long. The skeletons are sometimes preserved as fossils in rocks and can be easily recognized by their structure. Almost all corals today live at or near the equator, where it is always warm. Whenever you find coral fossils, even if they are in a cold climate today, you know that when the animals were alive, the climate was warm at that place. And although you found the fossils on land, the coral animals lived in the sea when they were alive.

Coal, another biogenic sedimentary rock, is made of ancient plants that accumulated in freshwater swamps. At the bottom of the swamp, the water was usually stagnant (didn't move). Trees that died and fell into the water accumulated because they did not rot away. Eventually they were covered by a thick layer of sand, and the pressure caused by the weight of the sand slowly changed them to coal.

The third group of sedimentary rocks are called *chemical rocks*. They usually form when seawater evaporates and leaves behind layers of the chemicals that were dissolved in it. For example, in a dry climate, a sandbar forms and cuts off a shallow bay along the coast. The water then evaporates and leaves a deposit of chemicals. If a storm washes away the sandbar, the bay fills with water again. When the sandbar forms again, the water evaporates and leaves a new layer of chemicals. This pattern repeats many times, so that a thick deposit of chemicals builds up. The salt that you use at home is one of the chemicals that formed this way. You can see for yourself how this process works. If you live near the ocean, get a jar of seawater and pour some into a saucer or soup plate. Leave it near a sunny window or some other warm place. As the water evaporates you will see minerals form from the dissolved chemicals. You can do the same thing with lake water or even water from your faucet, but the amount of minerals that forms will be smaller.

METAMORPHIC ROCKS ▪ *Metamorphic* rocks, the third group, are changed rocks. *Meta* means "change" and *morph* means "body" or "form." Any rock can change its form when enough heat is added and enough pressure is applied. The change happens because heat and pressure cause minerals in the rock to change their form and react with each other. These events result in a new kind of rock, a metamorphic rock.

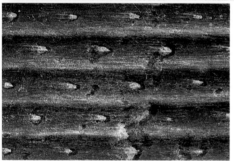

The round pebbles in this ancient conglomerate were deposited by rapidly flowing rivers.

The impression of a 300-million-year-old tree trunk is preserved in shale, a sedimentary rock.

This banded gneiss is metamorphosed sandstone.

The formation of the rock called schist provides a good example of this process. Pressure over a long period compacts the sediment clay and changes it to a sedimentary rock, shale. A small amount of heat and additional pressure applied to shale change it to a metamorphic rock, slate. Additional heat and pressure change the slate to phyllite and eventually to schist.

Limestone becomes marble through this kind of process. Granite becomes gneiss, which is usually composed of thick and thin, light and dark bands. These changes take place deep in the crust of the Earth. When you see metamorphic rocks, you know that erosion removed many miles of rock lying on top of them to expose them at the surface.

Rocks tell you about the geologic history of the place you live in. For example, if you find marble, you know it once was limestone that formed in shallow warm seas. Later the limestone was covered over with miles of newer sediment. Heat and pressure changed the limestone to marble deep below the surface. As the crust of the Earth moved upward, the layers on top of it were removed by the forces of erosion, and the marble was exposed. You can see now why it is important to be able to identify rocks.

THREE
THE ROCK CYCLE

The three main groups of rock—igneous, sedimentary, and metamorphic—may seem to be unrelated because of the very different ways they form. However, in the last chapter you saw how the sediment clay went through changes that finally transformed it into the metamorphic rock, schist. That is an example of how all rocks are interrelated as part of the rock cycle.

A good place to start looking at the rock cycle is with the story of igneous rocks. Although they are formed deep underground from molten material, after millions of years they may finally become exposed at the surface. There the forces of weather begin to work on them. Weathering causes rocks to fall apart. The force of gravity, which pulls everything to the lowest possible place, helps to move the loose pieces down slopes. In rainy places, water flowing down slopes also helps. Eventually, the pieces are carried to the bottoms of slopes where rivers transport the mud, sand, and gravel. Most of this sediment is carried to the sea, where it is gradually deposited in layers. As described in the last chapter, the increasing weight of the pile, over millions of years, compresses the older layers at the bottom, and minerals from the water squeezed out by this pressure act as cement. In this way pieces of igneous rock become sedimentary rock particles.

The layers of deeply buried sedimentary rock may be affected by Earth movements, which compress the rock and heat it, changing it to a metamorphic rock. The amount of heat and pressure determines the degree of change, or metamorphism. If the heat is great enough, the rock will melt. This molten material cools to form a new group of igneous rocks, completing a cycle.

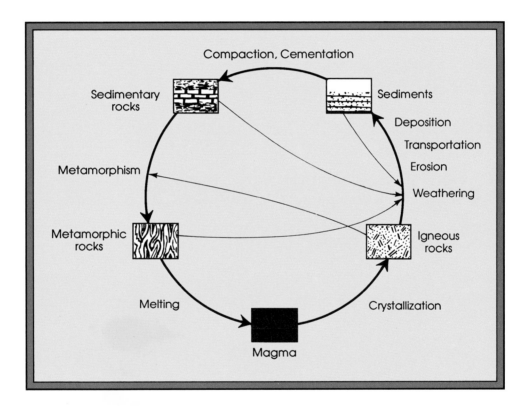

The rock cycle shows how the three main groups of rocks are interrelated.

But there are many variations to this story. Igneous rocks, especially plutonic types like granite, may be directly changed by heat and pressure. Sedimentary rocks may be crumbled by weathering, transported, and the pieces redeposited to form new layers of sediment. Metamorphic rocks may be exposed at the surface by *uplift* and erosion of the overlying layers, and the debris is deposited as sediments. These steps may be repeated over and over. It is important to remember that no loop in the cycle is more important than another.

Weathering is the first step in the breakdown of rocks. Two types of weathering affect rocks. Mechanical weathering breaks them into smaller pieces without changing their composition. Chemical weathering decomposes rock through chemical reactions, and changes the minerals in rocks to different minerals. Some minerals are not changed but are simply dissolved in water.

To understand weathering, try this experiment. Get some shiny new nails from home or a hardware store. Put one nail in a cup of water and keep it in a warm place. Put a second nail in another cup of water and store it out of the way in your refrigerator. Bury another nail in damp soil, and keep one nail in a drawer. If you find other places that are warm, cold, wet, or dry, put nails there, too. Once in a while check the nail that is in warm water. When it is good and rusty, label it to show where it came from and collect all the other nails. Make sure that you label them also.

You will find that some nails are very rusty and others are not. The nail that was kept driest has the least amount of rust, and the nails that were warm and wet rusted the most. This experiment shows that water is a chemical that reacts with other chemicals, such as minerals. It also shows that the type of environment—such as warm water or a dry drawer—affects how the mineral weathers. Water helps chemical reactions take place faster, and it can dissolve many substances.

The differences between conditions 10 to 15 miles (16 to 24 kilometers) underground and at the surface also cause chemical and physical changes in rocks. Minerals are stable in the conditions under which they form. When they form deep down and are brought to the surface by uplift, they become unstable. They may change their crystal structure, their chemical makeup, or both. Many minerals combine with water and oxygen to form new minerals. The new minerals are adjusted to their surface environment. Likewise, minerals that form on the surface become unstable when they are buried deeply. They, too, change into others as they adjust to their new environment.

Deep below the surface of the Earth, where some igneous rocks form, it is very hot and the pressure is very high. There is very little water or oxygen, and the rocks behave like clay or silly putty when they are squeezed. When these rocks reach the surface where temperature and pressure are low, however, they become brittle, and they crack and fracture.

Almost all rocks have cracks (also called joints or fractures). When water seeps into these cracks and freezes, it expands. The force created is powerful enough to break rocks, in the same way that pipes in a house burst when the water in them expands as it freezes. Plant roots also can split rocks. They start to grow in a small crevice and, as they grow bigger, make the crack larger.

Cracks allow chemical weathering to proceed faster. If you break a rusty nail, you will see that the inside still looks new. That happens because rusting, a kind of chemical weathering, starts on the surface of a substance and works inward. The more surfaces that are exposed, the faster the rock decays. To understand this process, take a cube of sugar and place it in a glass of cold water. Stir and watch the clock to see how long the sugar takes to dissolve. Then repeat the

The vertical cracks in the Palisades of New Jersey resulted from the shrinking of once molten rock as it cooled.

This Stone is erected
To the Memory of M: WILLIAM
ROGERS March. who departed
this Life on the 1. of October 1772
Ætat. 63:
In Him did shine the affectionate
Husband Tender Parent & kind Master

Tombstones show how fast rocks weather. Their dates tell us when they were new.

experiment, but this time crush the sugar cube. See how long it takes to dissolve. The crushed sugar takes less time because so many more surfaces are exposed to the water.

Weathering is a slow process. But you can see the results when you look at an outdoor statue. The figure may no longer look new because some of the details are gone and the lettering may not be clear. You can see the same effect in cemeteries. The inscriptions on some old tombstones may have disappeared completely.

We tend to think of weathering as a destructive process, but it produces one of the most important materials on Earth—soil. Different people have different definitions of the term "soil." To an engineer, soil is any loose material on the Earth's surface. To a farmer, soil is material to grow crops in. To a geologist, soil is weathered rock produced by the mechanical and chemical breakdown of rock. Creation of soil is one of the first steps in landscape evolution—the gradual change of the Earth's features.

FOUR
EROSION SHAPES THE LAND

Weathering is the rock breaker, and *erosion* is the rock mover. As the forces of erosion move rocks, they shape the land. Among the many forces that can move soil and rock particles, the most important are moving water, wind, glaciers, waves, and currents along the shore. Another erosive force that is always around us is gravity. Gravity pulls everything down to the lowest possible place.

GRAVITY ▪ Whether soil and rock particles are on steep or gentle slopes, they are always being pulled down by gravity. On the gentlest slope, the particles move downhill so slowly that you cannot see them move. Geologists call this movement *creep*. You can see the effects of creep on hillsides, where tombstones in a cemetery lean over, telephone poles are no longer vertical, and even houses slowly slide down. On steep slopes, rocks move down more quickly. This sudden movement is called a landslide.

When water soaks into the sliding material, the movement is called a debris slide or a mudflow, depending on the size of the particles. If gravity were the only force acting on the loose material, landslides would not occur as frequently as they do. When it rains, the extra weight of water makes rocks move down sooner. Water also acts as a lubricant. You can show how this works yourself. Get some sand and put it on a board. Raise the board slowly at one end, and

Different kinds of rocks weather at different rates. The stronger layers project more than the softer layers. Most of the weathered debris falls to the base of the cliff, forming a talus slope.

eventually the sand will slide off the board. Take note of how much you tilted the board when the sand started to move. Put the sand back on the board and start raising it again, but this time add a little water after you begin to raise it. You will see that the sand moves down the board with less tilting than was needed when it was dry.

Landslides start when some force puts rocks off balance. For example, when water freezes, the ice that forms in the spaces between rock particles can cause landslides. As the ice forms, it expands, pushing and moving the rocks. If this movement puts a rock off balance, gravity takes over and pulls it down. As the rock falls, it crashes into other rocks and starts them on their trip. The mass of rocks comes to a stop at the bottom of the hill or cliff, and the debris piles up. The loose rock that accumulates at the base of a cliff is called talus.

Growing tree roots can also push rocks apart. On steep slopes this action causes the rocks to move, and often the trees fall down with the rocks. Next time you look at a very steep slope, you will see that there are usually few trees.

Earthquakes shake loose rock off the surface and often cause huge amounts of debris to move into valleys. Sometimes the volume is so large that the slide blocks a river and creates a lake.

WATER ▪ After a rain, water flowing over the surface picks up particles. This slope wash eventually accumulates in channels on hillsides and turns into streams. The streams flow through low places called valleys. The slopes that dip toward the stream are called valley walls.

Streams and rivers are the most important forces of erosion. As streams flow downhill, they carry the rock debris with them. Small particles are carried in the water. Larger ones skip or roll along the bottom. All these moving particles scrape along the banks of the

**A river flowing on a flat surface meanders,
forming S-shaped curves.**

stream and the stream bed. This action causes the stream to cut downward, making the valley deeper. At the same time, rock debris moving down the valley's slopes widens the valley. In this way streams carve the land. Closer to sea level, streams often curve, or meander, back and forth. Streams meandering back and forth across valleys widen them by undercutting the valley slopes. While this is happening, the valley walls are becoming gentler, and the ridges that separate one valley from the next one are becoming lower.

Alpine glaciers are rivers of ice that deepen and widen river valleys.

GLACIERS ▪ In studying rocks, it's important to remember that climate changes through the ages. Sometimes it is hard to understand how a particular landscape formed until you realize that part of its development took place in a different climate. Glaciers provide a good example of this process.

Glaciers grow from snow that accumulates in cold climates. If some of the snow does not melt in the summer, it piles up year after year. As more snow falls, the snow below is packed down and eventually becomes a mass of ice, a glacier. Most glaciers form in high mountains and in polar regions. During periods when the Earth was cooler than it is today (the times we call ice ages) glaciers formed in places farther from the polar regions and moved farther down mountains.

Gravity pulls glaciers from high places to low places. As the ice moves, it picks up rock particles, which then become embedded in the base of the ice. These trapped rock fragments act like sandpaper as the glacier moves over rock surfaces, changing features that were formed earlier by stream erosion. A stream valley has a V shape. Glaciers deepen and widen the valley floor, changing its profile to a U shape.

As a glacier rubs against valley walls, it makes them steeper. This change causes landslides to occur. Rock debris from higher on the slopes falls onto the surface of the glacier, and the glacier acts like a sled as it carries this material away. Glaciers are also plows. They push rock material in front of them, forming a distinctive mound of rock debris. When the Earth warms again and the glaciers melt, all this loose material is left behind, forming a new landscape.

WAVES AND WIND ▪ You can study a hillside for years and not see any changes because erosion there takes place slowly. But along the seashore changes can be seen all the time.

Sit on a beach and watch the waves come in. The sand grains are continually shifting. Sand grains are carried away as water runs off the beach. The next wave brings new sand grains to the shore. As grains hit each other, they chip and get smaller. Currents along the shore carry the small grains away from the place where you are

**Storm waves etch away the weaker rocks
to form arches and solitary stacks.**

sitting. Waves bring them back to the shore farther down the beach. If you know which way the currents are moving, you will see that beach sand is finer in that direction.

Waves also crash into cliffs with enough force to break rocks, so that they fall into the water. The action of waves breaks up the rocks into smaller and smaller pieces, eventually into sand grains. This is the raw material that makes up many beaches.

Wind picks up small particles of sand and piles them up in dunes, usually parallel to the shore. Wherever there is a steady wind and loose material, you will probably see dunes. Sometimes the wind blows the sand hard enough to sandblast rocks, wearing away their surfaces. Like the action of running water and waves, wind takes loose material from one place to another and changes the shape of the land.

FIVE
ROCKS AND LANDSCAPES

Land is shaped by forces deep within the Earth and by weathering and erosion at the surface. These processes form all the Earth's landscapes, from high cliffs and jagged mountain peaks to gentle valleys and flat plains. Different kinds of rocks form under different conditions and are affected differently by erosion. As a result, certain rocks form particular landscape features.

VOLCANOES ▪ All volcanoes are more or less cone shaped and contain a crater, a small depression, at the summit. The cone forms because underground molten rock, or magma, rises to the surface through a narrow fissure, or *conduit*. As the molten material reaches the surface and erupts, most of it piles up around the opening, or *vent*.

There are about 500 active volcanoes in the world today. Volcanoes can remain active for tens of thousands of years. But that does not mean that they erupt all the time. Some volcanoes erupt once every 500 years. Some erupt at intervals for many years, then stop. Volcanoes that are inactive but can still erupt are called dormant, which means "sleeping." There are many inactive volcanoes that will never erupt again because the lava-producing activity within the Earth has shifted elsewhere.

When you examine the rock of a volcano, you may find that it is formed from lava or from ash or other, larger fragments. Most

Volcanoes are cone-shaped mountains built by the eruption of molten material. During this eruption, large blocks of molten material called bombs were thrown out of the volcano.

volcanoes that are built only of lava are called *shield volcanoes*, and they are usually found in the ocean. In fact, almost all oceanic islands are the tops of volcanoes. As the lava spreads out, shield volcanoes form broad-based mountains with gently sloping sides.

Volcanoes composed of layers of ash and lava are called *strato-volcanoes*, and they usually form on land, rising into tall, steep-sided cones. A volcano may eject ash during one eruption and lava during the next one, or the change may occur even during the same eruption. This is especially true for stratovolcanoes and explains why they are sometimes called *composite volcanoes*. ("Composite" means "made up of distinct parts.")

Eruptions help volcanoes keep their shape, because weathering and erosion begin to wear them away as soon as they form. The older a volcano, the less it looks like a cone—one way you can tell if a volcano has been active recently. Sometimes you have to examine the rocks to tell that a mountain is a volcano. Generally volcanoes composed of ash erode more rapidly than those made of lava.

The crater at the top of most volcanoes is small. But occasionally a volcano has a very large depression in its top. Such depressions, called *calderas*, form when volcanoes erupt very violently. So much molten material shoots out from beneath the volcano that the cone collapses downward into the emptied space.

Often the conduit that leads molten material to the surface is a long crack. When that happens, lava flows out onto the surface in great sheets, or lava flows. After they harden, lava flows are often resistant to erosion and form cliffs. Molten materials that do not reach the surface but spread out and harden between layers of rock are called *sills*. When exposed by erosion they also form cliffs. The Palisades of the Hudson River in New York and New Jersey are one of the best examples of a sill. These vertical columns formed as molten material cooled and shrank.

This waterfall flows over a strong layer of basaltic lava.

Deep below the surface, plutonic rocks cool and crystallize in huge masses called *batholiths*. In Greek, *batho* means "deep" and *lith* means "stone." Batholiths are frequently made of granitic rocks. Internal forces within the Earth raise the crust, and erosion eventually exposes the batholith. Weathering and erosion then shape the rock mass. Granite usually resists erosion and forms mountains that last millions of years.

CAVES ▪ Almost all caves and related features develop in limestone. This is because the mineral calcite, which makes up limestone, is dissolved by rainwater.

Water created this cave by moving through layers of limestone and dissolving them.

As rain falls, it picks up a gas called carbon dioxide from the atmosphere. The mixture of water and carbon dioxide makes a weak acid, carbonic acid. Rain soaking through the soil picks up more carbon dioxide, produced by bacteria and other organisms. That makes carbonic acid stronger. The acidic water moving through limestone beneath the soil dissolves the calcite and produces caves and many features related to them, such as *sinkholes*, underground rivers, and "lost rivers." The resulting scenery is called *karst topography*, named after a region in Yugoslavia well known for its large and beautiful caves. Caves found in a region that has a dry climate today were created when the region had more water. They show that the climate has changed.

Very often, water from above containing dissolved calcite drips through the cave roof and forms hard deposits that slowly build into *stalactites* and *stalagmites*. It's easy to remember which is which: A stalactite has the letter *c* and grows downward from the cave *c*eiling, like an icicle. A stalagmite contains the letter *g* and grows upward from the cave floor, or *g*round.

Like all other rocks, limestones have joints. Underground water moving through these fractures dissolves the surrounding limestone. As the joints in limestone enlarge, they extend to the surface. Sometimes a stream flowing on the surface will disappear as it flows into the wide joints and down into a cave. People sometimes try to find out where the stream comes out of the ground by adding red dye to the water. Sometimes the water travels a great distance underground, and the dye becomes so diluted that you can't see the red color. In this case, where the stream emerges remains a mystery. Sometimes the stream emerges on the side of a cliff and forms a waterfall. A large spring bubbling up from the surface may be a "lost river" emerging from the ground.

As caves enlarge, their roofs may become thin and collapse, forming holes at the surface called sinkholes. These sinkholes usually form quickly. In areas where buildings stand on limestone, homes sometimes have fallen into sinkholes. Many sinkholes fill with water, forming round ponds. Large numbers of sinkholes develop in karst regions; southern Indiana, for example, may have as many as 300,000 sinkholes.

When the process of dissolving continues further, many caves may join together. Then the entire roof structure sometimes falls in, creating large valleys called dry or blind valleys. Although there may be plenty of rainfall, these depressions are dry because almost all the water rapidly soaks below the surface through the enlarged joints in the limestone.

While almost all caves form in limestones, caves can form in a few other kinds of rock. Marble is metamorphosed limestone and also consists mostly of calcite. And like limestone, it is dissolved by water. Gypsum, or calcium sulfate, is a mineral that will dissolve in pure water, and some caves are found in rocks made of it, too.

In contrast, sandstone usually resists dissolving and other kinds of weathering, especially if the sand grains and the cementing material are made of the mineral quartz. Where different kinds of rocks are folded together into loops, sandstones frequently are left behind after less resistant neighboring rocks have been weathered and eroded. As a result, sandstone makes ridges and often the resistant top layer on mesas and buttes.

**Earth movements have folded these
layers of colorful sandstone.**

SIX

MOVING CONTINENTS

How rocks in the Earth's crust are raised to the surface, the way mountains form, and the reasons that volcanoes exist all relate to the structure of the Earth. What do we know about the Earth's interior? The deepest hole that has been drilled goes down about 6 miles (10 kilometers). When volcanoes erupt, they sometimes bring up molten rocks that formed 25 or 30 miles (40 or 50 kilometers) below the surface. But the distance to the center of the Earth from the surface is about 4,000 miles (6,400 kilometers). So you can see that geologists and other scientists who study the Earth have barely made a dent. To look at the Earth's inner structure, they have to use indirect methods. For example, earthquakes send vibrations through the Earth. Seismologists—scientists who study earthquakes—know from field and laboratory studies that these vibrations travel through different kinds of rocks at different speeds. By studying the records of these vibrations, they have constructed a picture of the Earth's interior.

INSIDE THE EARTH ▪ We know that the Earth is made of layers. The layer at the center, called the *core*, is divided into two parts, a solid inner part and a liquid outer part. The core is under great pressure and is very hot. The next layer is called the *mantle*. It is also very hot, but cooler than the core, and it has many layers. The cool outer layer of the Earth is the *crust*, which is made of continents and ocean floors.

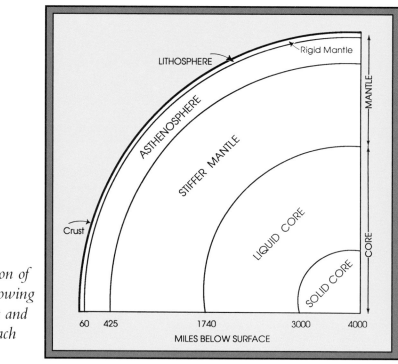

A cross section of the Earth, showing the thickness and names of each layer.

The crust and the solid outer layer of the mantle form the *lithosphere*. Directly below the lithosphere is the soft, semimolten *asthenosphere*, meaning "weak layer." Like the rest of the Earth's interior, it is kept hot by heat released as certain elements like uranium slowly change to different elements.

Geologists have discovered that the lithosphere is broken into about seven large and a number of smaller pieces called *plates*. A good way to picture the lithosphere is to look at an egg with a cracked shell. The eggshell stays together even with some cracks, but if a crack becomes too wide, some of the egg will seep out. On the "shell," or surface, of the Earth, however, the plates are moving.

The plates have irregular shapes with many edges. Movements along the edges are of three kinds: Neighboring plates may move past each other; they may move away from each other; or they may collide with each other, in which case one may dive below the other.

A plate may be made up of ocean floor or a combination of continent and ocean floor. As the plates move, so do the continents. This slow movement of continents from one place on the globe to another is called *continental drift*. It happens at the rate of about an inch a year, but over millions of years, the changes are significant.

CONVECTION CURRENTS ▪ What makes the plates move? All kinds of substances, from air to semimolten rock, become less dense when heated, and they rise. The semimolten rock in the asthenosphere moves upward toward the surface of the Earth, only to be blocked by the solid lithosphere. Because the rocks lose some of their heat as they rise, they become denser again, and they sink. During part of this circular journey, the semimolten material moves along the undersides of the lithosphere and causes the plates to move.

This circulation pattern of semimolten material is called a *convection cell*, and there are many of them in the asthenosphere. To get an idea of how convection cells work, think about a room heated by one radiator against a wall. The heat of the radiator warms the air around it. Because the warmer air is now less dense, it rises toward the ceiling. Cooler air near the floor takes its place. Air farther from the radiator then moves to take the place of the cooler air. In this way a circulation pattern is set up. The warm air rises to the ceiling, moves across the ceiling and, as it cools, drops down to the floor and moves to the radiator to be heated again. Soon the whole room is heated. You can see this pattern very clearly if someone in your house has the bad habit of smoking. If the smoker sits in one place, you will see the smoke rise and travel around in the same manner. That is how you get a smoke-filled room. Imagine that the air is moving semimolten rock in the asthenosphere and the ceiling is the bottom of the lithosphere, and you have an idea of what is happening in this part of the Earth's interior.

As mentioned above, the asthenosphere material moving slowly along the underside of the lithosphere pulls the lithosphere along. Where two convection cells move away from each other, the lithosphere is pulled apart. Where two cells come together, two plates collide, and one plate sinks below the other. All these actions take millions of years.

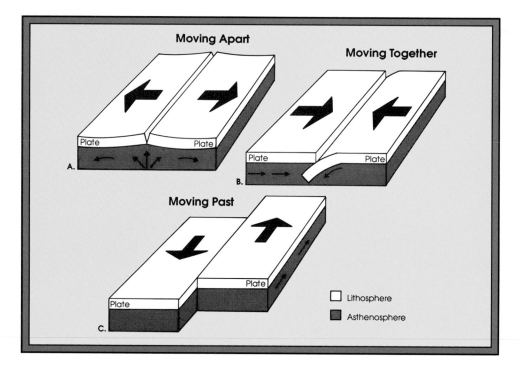

The three main kinds of movements along plate boundaries.

Contorted layers of rock result from earth movements. The vertical lines are drill holes for dynamite that blasted the rock away.

THE SEA FLOOR ▪ Under the ocean, where two plates move away from each other, a crack, or rift, forms. Molten rock rises into the crack, forming a mid-ocean ridge. When the molten material cools, it forms basalt. This rock is heavier than the neighboring continental rock, which is mostly granite. The basalt forms the new and enlarging ocean floor.

Geologists have found that the oldest rocks on the continents are about 4 billion years old, but the oldest rocks on the ocean floor are only 200 million years old. What happened to the older ocean floors?

They were destroyed at places where one plate sank beneath another plate.

Let's look at the Atlantic Ocean basin to see why ocean floors don't get older than about 200 million years. North America and Europe are moving away from each other at the rate of about one inch a year. The youngest rocks are forming now at the mid-ocean rift, and the oldest ocean floor rocks are next to the continents. The rocks at the rift are hot, but as the sea floor spreads, these rocks gradually cool and become denser. By the time they are 200 million years old, they are denser than the asthenosphere under the ocean crust and they begin to sink.

As the sinking oceanic plate enters the hotter regions it heats up, and friction from its movement adds more heat. This heat causes the plate to melt, and the molten rock will later rise to form volcanoes. When an ocean plate dives below a continent, the rising molten material forms volcanoes along the edge of the continent. Mount Rainier, Mount Baker, Mount St. Helens, and other volcanoes in the states of Washington and Oregon formed this way. If you look at a map, you will see that all these volcanoes lie along a straight line. That is because the nearby plate boundary is more or less straight.

Sediment that was eroded off the continent and carried to the ocean floor is returned to the continent by plate movement, too. As the plate dives under the continent, the sediment is scraped off, piles up along the continental edge, and forms mountains. This happens because the sediment is less dense than the surrounding rocks and can't be pulled into the Earth. It is a little like a rubber ball that will not stay under water when pushed down.

Millions of years ago, India separated from Africa and moved northward. It collided with the Asian continent and caused the sea sediments to be squeezed. Since rock lies below, the only direction

**The Grand Tetons of Wyoming were uplifted
along a series of faults.**

for the sediments to move was upward, to form folded mountains. The Himalayas, which include the tallest peaks in the world, formed as a result. You can visualize this action if you push a heavy rug from one end. The rug will be pushed into a series of folds. In the same way, mountains are raised as one plate approaches another and pushes the sediments into folds.

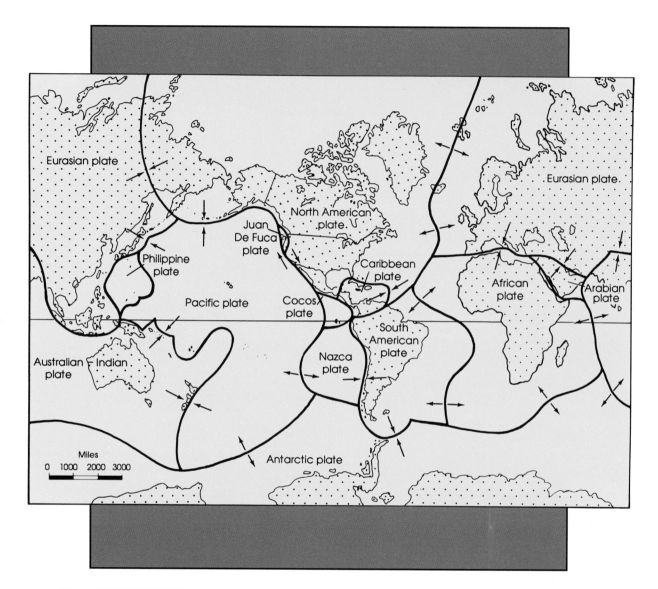

*The Earth's major lithospheric plates, showing how
they move in relation to one another.*

Sea floor spreading, moving continents, and other processes occur because the Earth is a great heat machine. The transfer of heat and material from one place to another causes all the major features we see on Earth. If the Earth did not have this internal heat, none of these things would happen.

The explanation of how the Earth "machine" works is called the theory of *plate tectonics*. In its modern form, it has been accepted by geologists since the early 1970s. It is as important as the theory of evolution is to biology, and it is an exciting field of study to be involved in. New discoveries are made all the time, and scientists rethink their ideas as a result. In this chapter we have only touched on some of the aspects of plate tectonics, but you can see that the Earth is continually changing on every level. And so is the theory of plate tectonics. As new discoveries are made, it will also evolve.

SEVEN
FOSSILS, LIFE OF THE PAST

Fossils are traces of ancient life, and the study of ancient life is called *paleontology* ("Paleo" means "ancient.") The term "fossil" comes from the Latin word meaning "dug up" because fossils are preserved in rocks and usually have to be excavated, or dug out. Sometimes a fossil is an actual shell or bone. It can also be a track or trail or even the preserved burrow of an animal. The excrement of ancient animals can be fossilized, too.

Because animals and plants live on the surface of the land or in the sea, fossils are found in sedimentary rocks, the rocks that form on the Earth's surface, or sometimes in rocks that formed from volcanic ash. You can imagine plants, animals, and even people trapped near a volcanic eruption. During an eruption gases are given off that can smother animals. The animals die and are covered over by the falling ash. You also might expect to find fossils beneath lava flows. As lava moves across the landscape, it buries whatever is in its path. But lava flows are so hot that they burn up anything caught under them. Plutonic igneous rocks like granite form deep below the surface, so you would not expect to find fossils in them. And the heat and pressure that produce metamorphic rocks—rocks that have been changed deep in the Earth—ordinarily destroy any fossils. If the amount of heat or pressure is not too great and causes only small changes, the fossils may be still recognized. But fossils found in these low-grade metamorphic rocks usually are bent out of shape.

A 360-million-year-old chambered shell of an extinct animal related to the octopus.

Brachiopods were abundant shelled animals that once lived on the sea floor and looked like clams.

It's hard to imagine how many trillions of animals and plants lived and died in the Earth's past, but fossils are rare in comparison. One way to understand why is to take a walk in the woods during the fall. Millions of leaves fall off trees to the ground. The wind blows them from place to place. As fall turns to winter, the number of leaves on the ground gets smaller. They are disappearing. Where are they going? They are disappearing because they are dry and break into smaller pieces, and because fungus grows on them and helps to destroy them.

How many birds do you see in a day? How about chipmunks, squirrels, and other wild animals? Do you see their skeletons frequently? No! That's because some of the animals die in burrows or hollows in tree trunks or other places where you would not ordinarily look. Wherever animals die, bacteria, fungi, and scavengers destroy the bodies rapidly. Animals that die in rivers are sometimes swept away, and their bones are ground up into small pieces. Along the seashore, waves and currents do the same thing. But in bays and lagoons, where nature tends to be more gentle, animals and plants have a better chance to be preserved. In fact, fossils of sea creatures are more abundant than fossils of land animals and plants.

For a plant or animal to become a fossil, it has to be protected from the biological and physical processes that would ordinarily destroy it after it dies. That may happen when it is buried beneath sediment or volcanic ash. However, even after a plant or animal is buried, the processes of destruction may continue. Bones and shells may be dissolved by water moving through the sediment. Sediments may be eroded and the skeletons destroyed when they are carried along by the water. When you go collecting fossils, you may see some rock layers that contain many fossils. They were probably preserved under unique conditions. Lots of sedimentary rocks show no trace of fossils. That is why a fossil hunter needs to have a lot of patience.

HOW FOSSILS FORM • Sometimes the process of fossilization begins at the surface. In fact, you can create these fossils in the same way as they are formed in nature. When you walk in mud, you leave the impression of your shoes or feet. When the mud hardens, you can still recognize the imprints of your shoe or toes. These imprints are called molds. Pour plaster of paris into one of the molds and, when the plaster hardens, you have a cast of the sole of your shoe or foot. Do the same thing with a seashell. Press it into mud, remove it, and pour plaster into the space.

In nature a shell can leave an impression on the surrounding mud. Sometimes the shell material slowly dissolves, leaving a space. Sediment or minerals fill in the space, creating a cast. To be preserved, the impression has to be buried under many layers of sediment. Even after burial begins, burrowing sea creatures like worms can destroy the impression.

Once a skeleton or a tree trunk is buried underground, water may deposit minerals in the tiny spaces, or pores, of the bone or wood. This type of fossilization is called *petrification*—meaning "turning to stone." In a related type of fossilization, called *replacement*, minerals in the skeleton are exchanged for the minerals in the water. Dinosaur bones are preserved by both of these processes.

Plants are usually preserved in marshes or swamps where they are covered over with mud. In this environment, even a leaf can make its impression in the mud as layers of new mud press down on it. All the chemicals that the leaf is made of disappear except the carbon, which remains as a thin film revealing the outline and structure of the leaf. Carbon is black. That's why many plant fossils have a black

Petrified wood shows the tree's growth rings clearly.

Left: A chambered fossil shell of a pearly nautilus, a relative of the octopus. Right: Trilobites, long extinct, were cousins of the horseshoe crab.

color. Where large numbers of fallen trees accumulate at the bottom of a swamp, they sometimes are covered over by sediments. Pressure and heat from the weight of the sediments cause chemical changes, and the tree material slowly changes to a material called peat. At this stage all the plant parts are recognizable. As heat and pressure increase, lignite coal forms, then bituminous coal, and finally anthracite coal. At the anthracite stage, the plant parts can no longer be recognized.

Here is something to think about. When you burn a piece of coal, you are releasing energy from the sun that was used by leaves to produce food so that a plant could grow. If the coal is 200 million years old, for example, you are releasing energy that has been stored in the coal for all that time. That is why coal is called a fossil fuel. Oil and gas are also fossil fuels.

When you dig something up, how old must it be to be called a fossil? Generally, if the specimen you dig up is more than 10,000 years old, it is a fossil. But there are exceptions, especially when you find remains of plants or animals that are extinct. Such specimens can be younger and still be called fossils. Some fossil hunters like to joke that if something you dig up smells, it is a biological specimen, and if it doesn't, it qualifies as a fossil.

How old can a fossil be? Fossils cannot be any older than the age of the first life on Earth. The Earth is about 4.5 billion years old. The oldest rocks found so far are almost 4 billion years old, and the oldest fossils date to 3.5 billion years ago. These fossils are bacteria and one-celled plants called algae, and you need special high-powered microscopes to see them. They were the most important forms of life on Earth for almost 2 billion years. During most of this time, the atmosphere contained no oxygen. But plants give off oxygen in the process of growth. As the algae produced more and more oxygen, it slowly began to build up in the atmosphere. When the oxygen reached a high enough level, animal life began to evolve very rapidly. It was only about a billion years ago that the great variety of life that we know on Earth today began to evolve. Fossils show us how life evolved through time on Earth.

Fossils also are used as tools by geologists to understand how the geography of the Earth has changed. They study fossils and the rocks where fossils are found to figure out which parts of the Earth were land and which were under the sea in the ancient past. The study of ancient landscapes is called *paleogeography*. Ancient animals and plants lived in their own particular habitats, just as animals and plants do today. Corals live in shallow tropical and subtropical seas, and dinosaurs were land creatures. Using information from many rock exposures of the same age, geologists can plot the ancient positions of land and sea on maps.

EIGHT

COLLECTING ROCKS

Collecting rocks, minerals, and fossils can be fun and very rewarding. You spend a lot of time outdoors, and you can meet many people who share your interest. Since it is very easy to gather a large collection quickly, you may want to limit the type of specimens you collect. It may be hard to decide at first, but once you begin you will find what appeals to you the most.

Minerals, fossils, and rocks each call for certain techniques to collect them and also to prepare them after you bring them home. But many of the techniques are the same for whichever you choose to collect. Rocks are probably the easiest to start with because you can see them in so many places. You can look for stones in driveways, in rock outcrops along the banks of streams, in the construction debris in empty lots, and in the piles of rocks in gravel pits. Minerals and fossils can be found only in certain kinds of rocks, and you will have to learn where to look for them in your area. Remember always to ask permission to collect on private property.

GETTING INFORMATION ▪ One of the first things you may want to do is to find out what you might look for in your neighborhood. Go to the public library and ask if there are any publications on the local minerals, fossils, and rocks. Quite possibly, someone has written about your area. Earth science teachers are also good people to ask

Examining specimens.

for information. You could also write to the geology department of the nearest college or university.

Most states have an office called the geological survey (sometimes called a natural history survey, or bureau of mines) that publishes or keeps files of collecting sites. These offices are usually located in the state capital. Often they publish geological maps, one of the most useful guides in helping you to find different rock types in your area. The United States Geological Survey also publishes numerous maps. You can write to them to find out if your area has been mapped.

Mineral or fossil clubs also give you useful information about collecting. Their members are very knowledgeable about where and how to collect specimens. Many clubs have monthly meetings and field trips. At these times you can get help with identifying specimens that you are not sure about and suggestions about how to take care of them. You will probably get a chance to trade specimens, too. You can't help collecting duplicates of some specimens, and you should keep those that are special or outstanding. Trading duplicate specimens is a good way to improve your collection, by swapping with another person who has specimens you cannot find. Some clubs have auctions or sales of specimens donated by members to raise money to help pay their expenses. They usually sell specimens at a low price, and you may manage to add hard-to-get specimens to your collection. Some clubs are open only to adults, but many members are happy to help young people. Many other clubs have a junior division.

You will also want to have books that will help you identify your specimens. Get suggestions from club members and teachers, and go to the library to look at the collection of books. Find out which books you can understand easily. Don't start with one that is too technical. Very often you can get older editions cheaply in stores that sell used books. The descriptions of individual rocks, fossils, and minerals don't change very much, but keep in mind that the scientific names of plants and animals may have changed. If you want a book that you can't find, ask if your library can get it through an inter-library loan program.

COLLECTING ▪ Now that you have information about local sites and reference books, it is time to go and collect. If you go by yourself, always let people know where you are going and how long you intend to stay at the place. Personal safety is very important. Wear good shoes for walking on rough ground, cover your arms and legs for protection against biting insects, if necessary, and bring insect repellent. If you are going to be away for several hours, bring food and drinking water and dress for the weather. Because you will probably be using a hammer and chisel to break rocks, it is wise to wear goggles to protect your eyes. These are also good precautions to take when you go with a group or on a club trip.

Collecting requires very simple equipment. All you will need at first is a rock hammer and a chisel to break rocks, paper to wrap the specimens so that they don't rub against each other, and a bag to carry them. If you intend to go to more than one place in a day, bring pen and paper. You can write the information about the site on a small piece of paper and wrap it with a specimen.

Professionals do not trust their memory as to where they found a specimen. They keep a notebook and use a number system for identification. For example, an entry in a notebook might be "1-1993 = Roaring Brook, Lakeside City, in stream at Jake Hammer's farm. A = rocks in stream bed. B = rocks in cliff below the

Some of the tools used to collect specimens. Also, you should wear goggles to protect your eyes.

Specimens are carefully wrapped so that they won't rub against other specimens and be ruined.

barn." You should also include the date of the collection, and you may want to note the weather or some other interesting fact. When you have learned enough, also describe the geological features of the site. This information will make your collection scientifically valuable in the future and help you remember the time you spent at the place. For example, new owners of a property may not want anyone to collect on their land, or a flood could erode the remaining outcrop or cover it over with river deposits. Sometimes an entire rock outcrop disappears because collectors took everything away. You will have accurate information about a site that is no longer available.

Don't spend too much time cleaning or trimming the specimens at the collection site, especially if it is a place you can't visit often or stay at for long. You will want to use all your time for collecting. If you find an interesting mineral or fossil that is partly exposed, take it home. There you will be able to carefully remove the unwanted rock under better conditions than in the field. Cleaning specimens in the field is usually uncomfortable, and you may feel rushed. That often leads to ruining a specimen.

Once home, sort out the specimens and decide which are best to keep for your collection. Also decide which specimens can be used for trading and which need further work to make the specimen look the best. The leftover specimens can be discarded, but find out if you can donate them to a school or give them to another collector.

After deciding which specimens you want to keep, begin the process of identifying the specimens. If you get stuck, ask someone to help you. If you can't identify a specimen right away, put it aside. As you learn more, you will eventually find out what it is. When you find a specimen that you think is very unusual and may be scientifically valuable, you should notify a scientist at a museum or university. If you can't take the specimen, send a photograph of it and a letter explaining why you think it deserves attention.

A typical museum label identifies a specimen and its locality.

Once you start identifying the specimens, you may want to give each specimen its own number in addition to the locality number. There are two general ways to keep the collection number. Some people like to paint a small area on the corner of a specimen with white enamel paint and write the catalogue number on it with black ink. You also can glue on a little sticker. Others make or buy boxes and keep each specimen in an individual box with a label listing all the information. If you use this method, you have to make sure that the labeled box and the specimen are kept together. At first, that may not be a problem, but as your collection grows it will be harder and harder to remember which specimen goes with which label.

For home study you may want to buy a hand lens or, if you can afford it, a student microscope. A 10-power lens is standard. The lens will enable you to examine small details on the specimen as well as aid you in cleaning it.

Rock collections usually need little preparation except for trimming. You may want to set some standard size for your collection, such as 2 by 4 inches (5 by 10 centimeters). All of your specimens can be trimmed to that size, with certain exceptions. Some features in rocks are large, such as folds in schist or colorful layers in sandstone. Specimens need to be larger than your standard size for these features to be seen.

Fossil-bearing rocks may require special attention. Very often a specimen needs to be cleaned. This is where your hand lens or microscope comes in handy. By working with the lens, you can make sure that you don't remove part of the fossil while cleaning it. Good tools are those that dentists use. During your next visit, ask the dentist not to throw away worn picks but to sterilize and save them for you. Some fossil-bearing specimens are very fragile and will eventually fall apart even if handled gently. The easiest way to protect a specimen is to coat it with clear varnish. Thin the varnish so that it can flow easily into the pores of the rock and fossil. Then examine the specimen to see if another coat of varnish is necessary.

You can use the same dental picks to remove the unwanted rock from mineral specimens. Because space to store specimens can be a problem, some collectors keep only tiny examples of minerals that can be seen clearly only under a microscope. Samples of any mineral, whether large or small, have the same properties.

A good way to organize a rock collection is by the major groups of rocks discussed earlier in the book. Fossils can be organized by kind, locality, age, or a combination of these characteristics. Minerals are usually arranged by their chemical makeup.

Just one more note about collecting. Rock exposures in many places are becoming rarer as more houses and shopping centers are built. Be respectful of the property where you go to collect. Land owners have closed sites because collectors left garbage behind, killed trees with their hammers and chisels, and painted graffiti on the rocks. Take only what you really want, so that the next collector will have something to collect. Collecting for the sake of collecting deprives people who come after you of the pleasure of discovering specimens.

Collecting rocks, fossils, and minerals is rewarding and fun. You learn about the Earth, the place you live in, and how it has changed through the ages. You will have an understanding of its continually changing nature. And you may even like rock collecting enough to become a geologist or a paleontologist when you get older.

GLOSSARY

asthenosphere—the semimolten layer of the Earth's mantle that lies below the outermost layer, or lithosphere.

batholiths—large masses of igneous rock that have hardened deep below the Earth's surface.

biogenic—originated or produced by life processes.

calderas—huge craters formed by violent volcanic eruptions.

chemical rocks—sedimentary rocks usually formed from deposits left by evaporation of water.

clastic—formed from the breakup of older rocks.

composite volcanoes—volcanoes formed of alternating layers of ash and lava.

conduit—a crack or fissure through which magma rises toward the surface.

conglomerate—sedimentary rock formed of hardened gravel.

continental drift—the slow movement of the continents.

convection cell—a circular pattern made by molten material as it rises, cools, and sinks.

core—the innermost layer of the Earth.

creep—the gradual movement of soil and rock particles down a slope.

crust—the outermost layer of the Earth.

crystal form—the outward pattern determined by the regular, repeating arrangement of the atoms or molecules of a solid substance.

dimension stones—rocks that are quarried and cut to specific sizes.

erosion—the wearing away of the Earth's surface by wind, rain, glaciers, and similar forces.

igneous—formed from molten material.

karst topography—a landscape with many caves and related features.

lava—molten rock that escapes from Earth's interior to the surface.

lava flows—sheets of lava formed on the surface of the Earth.

lithosphere—the solid outer layer of the Earth, made up of the crust and the outer part of the mantle.

magma—underground molten rock.

mantle—the middle layer of the Earth, between the crust and the core.

metamorphic—changed by heat and pressure within the Earth.

organic—containing carbon and hydrogen compounds produced by life processes.

paleogeography—the study of ancient landscapes.

paleontology—the study of ancient life.

petrification—a process through which minerals are deposited in the pores of bone or wood, creating a fossil.

plate—a section of the Earth's lithosphere.

plate tectonics—the theory that forces within the Earth cause the plates to move, creating continental drift and other changes in surface features.

plutonic—formed from molten material that solidified deep below the surface.

replacement—a process through which minerals in water replace minerals in bone, creating a fossil.

sandstone—a sedimentary rock formed of hardened sand.

sedimentary—formed from sediments, such as clay, sand, and gravel.

shale—sedimentary rock formed of hardened clay.

shield volcanoes—volcanoes formed of lava.

sills—sheets of molten material that have cooled below the surface.

siltstone—sedimentary rock formed of hardened silt.

sinkholes—depressions created when the roofs of caves collapse.

stalactites—mineral deposits that grow downward from cave ceilings.

stalagmites—mineral deposits that build up on cave floors.

stratovolcanoes—volcanoes formed of layers of ash and lava.

uplift—the raising, by internal forces, of a section of Earth's crust.

vent—the opening of a volcano, through which lava escapes.

weathering—the physical and chemical alteration of rock by wind, rain, and similar forces.

FURTHER READING

Diagram Group and David Lambert. *The Field Guide to Geology.* Facts on File, 1988.

Roma Gans. *Rock Collecting.* HarperCollins Children's Books, 1987.

Meish Goldish. *What Is a Fossil?* Raintree Publishers, 1989.

Sidney Horenstein. *Familiar Fossils of North America.* Knopf, 1988.

Terry Jennings. *Rocks & Soil.* Childrens Press, 1989.

David Lampert. *Rocks and Minerals.* Franklin Watts, 1986.

Christopher Lampton. *Volcano.* The Millbrook Press, 1991.

S. Mayes. *What's Under the Ground?* EDC Publishing, 1989.

Jenny Wood. *Caves: An Underground Wonderland.* Gareth Stevens, 1990.

INDEX

ABOUT THE AUTHOR

*Sidney Horenstein is a geologist and
coordinator of environmental public programs
at the American Museum of Natural History
in New York City.*

*He is well known for his educational tours
of the city, which point out ancient geological
features in the midst of the modern activity.*